www.finishinglinepress.com

THE JUKEBOX WAS THE JURY OF THEIR LOVE

poems by

Rodney Torreson

Finishing Line Press
Georgetown, Kentucky

THE JUKEBOX WAS
THE JURY OF
THEIR LOVE

Publisher: Leah Maines
Editor: Christen Kincaid
Cover Art: Johan Vander Tol
Author Photo: Steve Fortugaleza
Cover Design: Elizabeth Maines McCleavy

Printed in the USA on acid-free paper.
Order online: www.finishinglinepress.com
             also available on amazon.com

Author inquiries and mail orders:
Finishing Line Press
P. O. Box 1626
Georgetown, Kentucky 40324
U. S. A.

Table of Contents

for Phil Hey, there for me since the beginning

Catching What's Cool: Holiday Inn in Okoboji, Iowa

I'd catch the cool of "It's Not Unusual"
bucking the jukebox in the bar,
of Tom Jones himself, who always sounded
right *there*, shining behind his golden tenor.
But for in-house cool, it was Pete the Bartender,
though no girls, as far as I knew,
threw panties at Pete like they did at Tom Jones
from the audience of his TV show.

Pete's smiles, meted out easily as gin and tonics,
took nothing from him. In golf slacks and cardigan,
it was not unusual for Pete's calming presence
to put things right, like that time two bellicose men
cashed in their shadows for martinis—
madcap strings of them. On the other hand,
it was not unusual for Trudy, the other barkeep,
to shift into work with a hostile strut of high heels,

a sigh that started in her eyes and picked up
breath, and it was not unusual
for me to try to be strictly dining room,
my job description, when Trudy was around,
though she'd motion me into the bar,
her nose raised, her flared nostrils
doing the thinking as to what she might do
to wear a boy down. But with a wink

Pete would restore me, easy does it, as he'd pull
a Schlitz or Michelob from the cooler
or taking a shot glass between finger and thumb,
soften its glare, who'd seek my help by poking his head
through the window linked to the dining room.
Elbows on the counter, he'd catch my eye
with a shiny half dollar plucked from the register,
get me to wash glasses, a dirty dozen he could have easily

washed himself. Coin in hand, it was not unusual to be cool

on my way to the jukebox, feel suave as Tom Jones,
while I imagined a certain girl coming between me
and the Wurlitzer to punch in "F1"—so close her bare
shoulder blades roamed my fingertips, me believing

along with the song that I could be "loved by anyone,"
knowing all it takes is one guy and his girl
rubbing up together for a lifetime, making a pearl.

I.

The Jukebox Was the Jury of Their Love

Attentive quarters slipped into their slots,
the Temptations with "My Girl,"
the Zombies, "Time of the Season,"
in his girl's eyes derision,
though the jury was still out.

His palm on the bible of her hand
promised to tell the truth, but he was edging
back from rumors how he'd caught
some girl up against
the pool table, and the two of them
got lost in the coat rack.
"Liar, Liar," called Three Dog Night,
as he hung his head, his girl crying
on someone else's dime.
Oh, yes, her coin—he remembered now
her quick trip to the Wurlitzer in her mini,
adjusting the belt, so it fell closer to the knee,
her righteousness worked out
in a sense of modesty
she never had while they had dated.

Now she was weeping for herself,
not this dumb guy who'd walk
her right out of this small town
through the Box Tops' "Neon Rainbow"
and into the "city night,
the pretty lights" as if after high school
it would save their souls.

And now the song was spinning again—
with his girl coming on slow, having
bought off the jury with another quarter.
In their slow crawl, he finally
felt her fingers upon the sentient galaxy
of his wrists, and what would you know?—
now spun the Buckingham's cover

of Cannonball Adderly's
"Mercy, Mercy, Mercy."

In St. Louis, My Son, Daughter
and I Stroll the Old Delmar Loop

where, at 84, Chuck Berry still shakes out an appearance
one Wednesday a month. But it's Saturday night
beneath the big, bare moonbeams
where my heartbeat meets the stamp of the street
and brass plaques embedded in the sidewalk
for Berry, Miles Davis, Sheryl Crow and others.

We brush by two girls with the bruised-blond look,
hear the sidewalk shouts of two men a block apart
on this—"One of the Ten Great Streets in America,"
one guy yelling, "Hey, Man, I'm locked out!"
the other, "No shit!—it's the second time today!"
Dusk drains into our footsteps, reaching its depths
when I shoot a glance down an alley,

sure at some point, a knife has tried to remove a wound,
hear a girl, mid-teens, rating every young man
passing by, me in the middle, between
my son and daughter, as she screeches,
"Gawd, no, he's too old!" Primed with good vibes,
I recover a few to swing open the door
of the Blueberry Hill. A man shows us to a table.

The walls are dressed out in old concert posters,
the hall to the bathroom in photos
of the proprietor with every musician
from Keith Richards to Solomon Burke and John Hartford.
And at a table, tapping a foot to non-stop oldies,
it is suddenly Wednesday down in the Duck Room,
standing room only, and I'm there in raw applause,

rising as Berry steps from a shadow with his Gibson,
starts its engine and breaks into "Johnny B. Goode,"
as tax evasion and other misconduct try to tower over him
bent at the knees, but Chuck Berry plays no conflicted chords

in his duck walk, as the song finds its fire bed,
and it is 1956, and I'm five years old at the bedrock,
and afterwards on the street again, the girl who's rating young men
looks at me as if I'm some kid and grins.

Brian, the Calendar is in Shadow
in the Beach Boys' New Album

I fit all my teaching—thirty-six years—
between the last two LPs to receive rave reviews—
while, Brian, often obese beneath a bathrobe,
you fit two of your three breakdowns.
As I retire and ponder your puffy planet
where no birds stirred, the Beach Boys' new album,
That's Why God Made the Radio, is what one critic
says has no business sounding this good.
Still, with your concession to getting along
(like mine for putting those years behind me),
some of the LP never made it, Brian,
to the inside of your custodial heart.

For, like a kiss too controlled for passion,
the rest is rife with Mike Love's patterns
built around hot rods and the beach,
which should have gone the way of outfits.
Still, wonderful wheels of harmony persist,
circling in the air of this long player.
I remember years ago, the Beach Boys reduced
to a road band, with studio work sparse,
you stayed home, your refuge a sandbox.
In the new publicity shots, I look in your eyes
for ground clouds or the attic,
as when you were embraced by shrink wrap,
not even wearing the prescribed smile.
May green vines spiral into your isolation.

Sometimes in my teaching I was out of it too:
overly medicated and with worn-out plans,
with coffee stains on the carpet
showing how homely, how pedestrian,
were my moves. In this new album
the calendar is in shadow, the clock is too,
with Father Time somewhere in white tennies,
trying on the old white Levis and striped shirts.

Sprite rhythms and the flying surf of "Isn't it Time?"
recall "Do It Again," and I swing back to my first year
teaching poetry—junior high kids impulsively rising
from their seats, applauding what E.V. Griffith
in *Poetry Now* labeled "Other People's Flowers."

The new album has few weedy revelries.
Some of the songs like my years in the classroom
are sometimes bland between the high, over-
arching parts. Old Brian, older than me, I imagine
your muse still painting California girls,
sweeps of curve wading a shimmering surf,
or in Malibu a girl stepping down
from the headland with the help of her
brown trusted toes. Though fog hangs
over Malibu, there is no haze in the harmony.

How you collaborated with hanging shadows
from the calendar, your harmonies pure,
none of the voices after fifty years
a ramshackle mansion; you and the surviving Beach Boys
sound strangely young, the last song, "Summer's Gone,"
on likely your last album, ends with waves
that nearly chime, an immaculate refrain,
perhaps the rustling of gulls, no gritty epiphany
like my year of retirement from other shadows.

Since You Always Threw Yourself Out There, David Ruffin

in that drizzle called life, such as onto the stage
for that impromptu audition with the Temptations,
maybe in the end, it was easy for NBC
in the mini-series to throw the facts about.

Framed by your trademark black glasses,
while the other Temps danced a labyrinth behind you,
you would whirl around, throwing the microphone up
with one hand, snatching it with the other,

then hitting the floor with a leg split so crisp
that before you'd rise, the other Temps saw
the fortune of the moon and stars breaking your way,
your extended hand offering it to the crowd.

In the sun's turn-around time, you'd lunged
into stardom. Or maybe after the opening riff—
with its climbing guitar notes that scaled the heart
you flung yourself into "My Girl,"

which Smoky Robinson wrote just for you, your baritone,
that gritty scuffle, going sweet as water over stones,
so that 700 miles from there in Terril, Iowa, cold wind
at our ribs, the song would strike up a blue sky:

"I've got sunshine on a cloudy day / and when it's cold outside, /
I've got the month of May," my brother Dean,
while the wind was reduced to a few breezy spumes, rigging
speakers in our upstairs window, so we could broadcast

"My Girl" all over the block—teaching it to the trees,
the flowers, even the crusty, world-weary sidewalks,
as if their cracks could take on your other trademark—
that break in your voice, so that even Beryl Coleman,

the old no-nonsense justice of the peace, who lived next door,

would take store of your song, and her drapes would sway,
though back in Motown, you were leaping into arrogance,
traveling solo in your mink-lined limo, while the rest of the band

hit the turnpike in a station wagon, with you going so far
as to have your glasses painted on your limo,
as you hurled yourself into everything but rehearsals,
which you'd miss along with, later on, the concerts,

in your drug-induced exile, all this leading to a hiss
in your skillet that broke the crying stillness,
and frost on the furniture, and you trying
to sign away your lady friend's Lincoln Continental

for $20 of cocaine, the Temptations soon voting you out
of the group. It was *then*, ironically, you'd show up
at gigs, flinging yourself onto the stage—for the shiny ache
you cosseted—while, for the Temptations

the stage lights stung, the audience weighing in with applause
when you'd pry the mike from the new front man's hands,
for "My Girl" or maybe "Ain't too Proud to Beg"
or "Beauty's Only Skin Deep" or "I Wish It Would Rain."

And, my God, did it rain! The boiling truth of it
is you died in a Philadelphia crack house,
the limo driver then escorting you to a hospital.
Instead NBC tossed you out with the trash,

so that beneath the strain of streetlights, fans saw
your body being flung from a car into the ashen traffic,
as if it were only what you deserved,
and a funeral parlor pillow was all that you were after.

Hitchhiker

To remain unmoved
on this frigid Nebraska road
the couple accelerates past the hippie
on their way back
to Iowa, the young man's thumb
with no luck to grow
a garden of love
nor sprout a good turn
beneath that looming hardtop.
The couple not to divide
their hearts for long hair
and rags to get close again
to that strange vibration—
the 'Frisco song
about "flowers in your hair"
they thought they'd
not miss. But the wife says
as they barrel by, "Suppose
he was ours?" and the husband:
"Yes, we'd like to believe
the world would stop." And behold
when they grumbled
tires to the shoulder, straining
beyond their reach
and backed up, they sprout
into the woods of that face.
Out of the car, he slides
around the fenders and finds—
to the thaw of the heart-bitten—
she already raising by the chin:
hollows, ridges of a face,
a shadow fully fleshed
stretched in a kiss.

You're 18, Riding with Friends to a Record Store

in Dylan's old haunt of Dinkytown
and know that ten years earlier Dylan was your age,
living there, the world still unsorted.
And above Gray's Drugstore
in a room with a window that shrunk into an alley a view,
the name Bob Dylan is a whisper that blooms.
You ride by the Victorian houses, feeling him maybe
in wind off a balcony, glimpse him
in the juggle of renters. Yes, riding with friends
with an eye out for the shape of absence,
Dylan as you sensed him after
his motorcycle accident. If you could spot him
under the hiss of electric lines in a bare alley,
he'd possess, surely, the cosmos in his eye.
In crisp October, you feel the bite of his lyrics
still on the loose and yet to be leveraged
into a song. You think about how
months after his arrival he left for greatness
in the middle of a snowstorm.
A churlish cigarette, maybe, drew him in
and he was gone, and you in Dylan shoes
try to rent shadows, creating your own windup myth,
in Minneapolis, where you'd have put his footprints
in a picture frame if you'd found any,
where Dylan and Dinkytown are mentioned
in the same breath, in the melody of rumors,
where maybe he spidered his lips across a blues harp
at The Ten O'clock Scholar.

1969

You touch that new beginning you never
worked up that summer the songs
simmered on the jukebox at the Bluebird,
its pretty waitress in the rhythm of her orders,
a stranger once again, as you walked up
to the sliding screen, only you and the light bulb
above us enthralled as she took your order, her eyes
wide seas but without the old undertow
to pull you in. It took you back to Cokes
you had with her each day at a restaurant after school,
you never learning until the Ouija spirit spelled your name
it was of you that she dreamed, her cousin's eyes wide
with the rightness of the board.
By that time, it was over, no fermenting kiss.
After that the jukebox killed you off,
as the Zombies sang about "pleasured hands,"
and yours held nothing but a coffee cup.
And you kicked yourself for taking her to love
and not even knowing it, as at the table
"It's the time of the season for loving" left you
with little but fighting off mosquitoes
and picking over the blighted fries, and learning
that ice cream has shadows too,
when you never felt so alone,
as you dropped another dime in the Wurlitzer,
that wishing pond.

With the Hard Band Rocking Off for the Weekend

I stayed alone at the house on Crime Street
in an expansive time drawn out and drummed in
by the riddle of how I'd wound up in such a dump.
Contracting floorboards had formed pyramids,

which loomed larger than the sum of their boards.
too high to step over, we had to walk around them.
In our kitchen with its vast pyramid and congested
traffic pattern, we were eight rowdies pushing our way

around, each of us in turn raising a chicken leg in jest
to beat the others back. But on the weekend—
with all the bravado gone—I was alone, matching wits
with midnight, for l was too alert, too there,

ears open to every door. I had developed a mild case
of omnipresence and could exert myself into every room
at once, hear every sound, though I could not determine
its source. Then a cabbie was killed, scooped in our alley,

and a clerk at the corner store disappeared in an aisle mirror.
Thieves had run ladders to the second floor of our house,
then handed down guitars and the dismantled constellations
of drum sets, while the band jammed downstairs.

I'd been seeing the ghost mother of Jeff, a boy
I worked with, every night the last one of her life lived
over and over in what had become my bedroom.
I would watch her frenzied strip routine before she'd

leap out the window, taking most of the fire with her.
With her son, I worked fast food, passing burgers
through holes in safety glass. A co-worker helped me
put it all together, telling me when he drove me home

after work, "That's where Jeff lived up through the fire."
I was often apart from even the girl who for a short while

was enthralled with me, and who drove by the house
one night at 2 a.m. A thief as well, she took too much of me.

As we kissed, she'd close her lashes over my eyes,
blind me to all others in that year of "Killing Me Softly."
The soft rock of that year had turned me soft, too,
leaving me afraid of the dark. When my girl with her friend

drove by to check on me so late that it was morning,
she likely saw me as weak, for all the house lights
were lunged on. Outside loitered men with hard bands
of their own, their arms totem poles of watches,

men who had so much time on their hands
that they must have known when I'd roll over in bed
and step up to the glassy pupils we call windows
to watch for everything from threadbare birds

to nippy Ripple bottles being emptied on our lawn.

For Janis, Who Shouted Out Entire Canyons in Her Songs

I'm a victim of my own insides. There was a time when I
wanted to know everything...

Janis Joplin

What Janis behind her granny glasses knew
as she belted out "Kozmic Blues,"
her hands wringing out the last smidgeons
of lift from the embroidered tablecloth
she wore as a dress was there are questions
we can never come back from once
we've asked them. It all comes back
to what we remember neatly sawed
and stacked like timber suddenly coming undone
and being flung out into the universe.
Breathing full-mouthed at the cavernous
mike and flagging cosmic matter
Carl Sagan only dreamt about, she'd cry,
"I keep movin' on, but I never found out why,"
while flashing before her the ugly
man contest she won but never
entered in college, now hurling
her blues higher, way out beyond
those dismissive of roses until,
for an instant, the blues give up
in her grasp, echo her whimper dying
to that monster of silence, her love raw,
full to the tipping point of her breasts.

The Strange Pact between Gram Parsons
and the Manager of the Flying Burrito Brothers

Parsons is dead at 26, and Kaufman and a crony
wearing "Sin City" jackets and unwieldy stares—
cast in the stone of alcohol and fear—pull up
at the airport in L.A. Near a flatbed,
they park their hearse. Its busted windows
and empty license plate marquee show death
does not fuss with small concerns. Under skewed
cowboy hats they honor commitments
with wild-eyed lies about being hired
to whisk Gram Parsons' bones to another airport.

To their surprise, the driver of the flatbed
believes them, turns over the corpse, despite
Kaufman's quip: "We're on overtime
and we've got a date with a couple of hot broads.
Give us the stiff." There's lifting of the body—
a most modest resurrection—before they
set him down in the old black hearse.
Soon they're off on desolate roads—
far from the belly crowds in bikinis—
in a flighty thrill that rivals
Parsons' in the motel, trespassing over
the boundaries of pleasure—a trip
wayward as his vocal and strung-out guitar
which painted misery with an aching shimmer.

Kaufman, creeped out, thinks how one corpse
can surround you on every side,
but they have their instincts, driving
their friend's body to his resting place—
wary that Parson's corpse may do something foul
like open the lid, sit up, and with a pale hand
on the frilly rod make a curtain call.

On they drive, with cacti their horizon,
rescuing themselves with beer and Jack Daniels,

making it to the desert's dry resolve,
where under the stars they grapple
with the casket. Kaufman opens it
and pours in 5 gallons of gas,
touches Parsons' chest, then with a match
flicks his hand at the face, his dissuaded hair.
He and his hippy friend laugh,
as a fireball blasts a mile into the sky.

And as the hearse squeals off, they imagine
Gram's spirit bequeathed feathers to flap about
the Joshua tree. The police car that soon chases
doesn't slug along but must follow taillights flying
wildly from liquor sparked by wise cracks—
as Kaufman would later say, not being encumbered
by sobriety was why they got away.

On My CD of *Pussy Cats,*
You Never Stop Singing "Don't Forget Me"

and it's me always answering, "Not ever, Harry,
no matter how much the future stews."
A dozen years after your overcrowded heart
gives out, I long for your four octaves,
when you were your own choir,
your voice scaling every wall,
yet so intricate it pieced
together even the shadows
broken over the heads of flowers.

Of course, that was before you
recorded *Pussy Cats* in the middle
of a sore throat that blew up in slow mo,
so that the explosion caught sides
of so many songs,
vocal chords besmirched forever
so that at the end you were but a stitch
in the culture for those
who only knew "Without You."

But how I miss you, Harry! For in you
we felt the breath of moonbeams
"as they danced around the weathervane,"
your sweet vocals not airbrushed
as a feature of the breeze
at odds with your profane occasions
that kept me from showing
all your vinyl sides,
though they made circles.

Harry, your soaring vocals
could take me out of the mouth
of the couch or put me into it,
as I carefully listened, as if
you were tussling with light.
You could fill your voice to the brim

or turn it over to adjust splendor
or shape the rain, so it would come loping
across our hearts or make a lake squirm
in your loneliness, suddenly mine,
or reap chaos in a song like "Jump into the Fire,"
a place I'd let you go to alone.

Apartment: Myron, Leonard Cohen, and Me

Though Leonard did not pay rent,
it was what Myron termed
Leonard's groan across guitar strings
that upset him, as Myron feared his girlfriend
would break things off, if she realized
his roommate was such a buffoon
that he'd like listening to what Myron called
nasal drips caught up in Cohen sucking
up. Myron would whine that I played
old Lennie boy so much (his words, not mine)
he might as well have his name on our mailbox.
God forbid she hear him answering
as she mounted stairs to rap on our door.

It must be said—Leonard asked for nothing,
not even a bed, for by now
Leonard's life was even more Spartan
than in *Songs from a Room.*
The spindle, a lit candle, centered the turntable,
kept his spirit warm—in this,
his summer away from Marianne—
a time when he renounced his skin.
What most upbraided Myron
was coming home to Leonard's incessant drone:
"A Bunch of Lonesome and Very Quarrelsome Heroes."

Later, while Myron stunned his woman
with the grandeur that is man,
I'd sit in the living room
with Leonard's exquisite offerings of song,
where I'd give his records a whirl and then another
as he'd lean upon my life with his silky dark,
the top of the record stack
Leonard's little joke, since nothing
was ever surface about Leonard.
Sometimes, we'd wander the bleak alley
for hidden beauty, his spirit surrendering

brooding flowers, while I lumbered behind him
with a muse not mine, carrying his song.

After the Rehearsal We're at Rex's Roadhouse in St. Paul

where saddles hang from the rafters,
lassos brand the menus. If my friend Ken's
feeling roped into this marriage, he doesn't show it,
as he impersonates his profs at med school,
gets us laughing so hard our heads
are almost under the table
before coming up for air. But, later, behind
the restroom door, with its hearts and spades
and interlocking six-shooters,
Ken and me at the urinals, he stares at the wall
and says, "I won't be at the church tomorrow.
Do what you want—stay away or show up."

I feel like we're the bad guys at the O.K. Corral
in a shootout with the Earp brothers.
"You should tell Ellen," I tell him
but wash my hands of it. "I can't," he says,
then it's rock' n roll, with Ken drumming
the towel dispenser, singing the Bee Gees,
the song he'd wail and knuckle the table to
at the campus canteen when we were undergrads:
"I gotta get a message to you. Hold on, hold on.
One more hour and my life will be through,"
he sings through a grin.
.

Ken's only message, though, is for me,
as I cringe for Ellen's family from Brooklyn,
friendly folks, not a woolly eye among them, who'd close
the great divide between the Midwest and the coast.
But the next day, without ceremony,
Ellen's plopped on the floor of the church vestibule,
family circling her in the aching off-limits,
her dress, hopped up on frills, looks more for mopping
than a sweep train. But I'm still standing,
hands in my pockets through rapid-fire silence,
pretending to know nothing.

Little Stevie Wright, Easybeat Frontman,
Before You Got Your Own

you and the band rocked me with electric
shock treatments, though mine were pure wonder
that summer day at Burr Oak Lake,
after my teenage mood wound the cloud up
on my reel to fish radio, "Friday on My Mind"
coming on like torpedo fish that the Romans used,
electric and eel-like, to pluck patients from a funk,
the song moving way out in front
of me to meet the girl you sang about, Stevie,
a sinker beat, a two-note staccato intro,
then the band's gutter guitar with your slow
rising vocal climbing to a shout:
"Cuzz I have Friday on my mind"—
which socked me with adrenalin of love
someday mine, making me cooler than I was.
Even when things went wrong, something in me seemed
free and flowing as ivy on a wall
until the whole wall falls,
enough for my shimmering ache of being 16
when I didn't have a girl
and drove a Corvair around town,
trying to ride the potholes to glory, half expecting
that one of the jolts might slip
the calendar's loose summery grip,
you already too electric, so doctors
gave you shock treatments:
civilized thunder and lightning,
then sleep therapy, and when summer's curtain closed,
the song reverberated all fall and winter,
the numb weekdays of classes drummed away,
the drudgery of hallways, "Friday on My Mind"
granting my soul all the free passes it would need.
But for you, Stevie, it was not enough.

In the Back Seat, Leaving the Green Mill with Friends

Tonight, her fiancé in 'Nam,
her svelte arms drowning,
she, his blind side exposed,
murmurs in the St. Paul cold,
"Hold me,"

the radio playing the Mamas & Papas.
No "Go Where You Want to Go" anthem tonight
but "Dedicated to the One I Love":

"When I am far away from you, my baby,
whisper a little prayer for me, my baby…"

"Hold me," she repeats,
her knees pulled up—hard friends
to her chin, shivering,

her fiancé maybe dodging a grenade
while she goes off at home.

"Just hold me."

Our cheeks, fumbling, strike a match.
We kiss deep—but hold *him*.

From London the Beatles Board Pan Am 101

and don their plane faces
but for laughter, nervous and unfastened.
No gritty epiphany, though
they've shed Hamburg and leather jackets,
as Heathrow shadows yield to "Yeah, yeah, yeah,"
and the Beatles are coming to America
through a shiny pocket in the day,
as stateside girls dream of "I Want
to Hold Your Hand"
and squeal for a luminous knot—
the thought of forming one with a lad
under a mop, of carrying it
between them as they stroll the park.

Landing, their wit digs in with the wheels,
these Beatles now a door for the young,
exit the plane, turn and wave
to the crowd in unison.
In the terminal the journalists press:
"Are you going to have a haircut
while you're in America?"
No eyeroll from John to jeopardize
the tipsy floor mikes,
"I had one yesterday," George quips.

They sleep at the Plaza
in an offbeat suite just off
flashbulb fever. Two days later, the night
on Ed Sullivan rises to meet them,
and, after the cue, not one
of the Beatles flinch from exuberance.
And tonight, months before
the shadows they have denied
sweep over them, before they yield
to a deeper bed of song,
they're delightfully tepid in ties and mohair suits,
their vocals shiny as medallions,

as they chime sanded harmonies
on "All My Loving," wield guitars
through "She Loves You," and Paul and John
shake out a wooo. Though there are no
beastly riffs, Ringo makes mincemeat
of the drums; the girls choose from their repertoire
of screams. And all over America,
on TV sets everywhere, George and John catch
each other's eyes, as they net the girls
in their quiet bangs—lairs for hysteria,
and all over America the Fab Four find favor
even with the melody police
who grew up on Glenn Miller.

Beneath a Black Sun Jerry Lee Lewis

his Tennessee hills not far
behind, tries to clear way
for a child bride:
"I marry who I damn well please!"

His new songs don't get played.
"Great Balls of Fire" inspires
fresh alarm. Fans abandon him
as if suddenly "Whole Lotta Shakin'..."
gets personal—as if he'd been
grabbing fans
by the neck,
his back of
hand slapping them
down a row of keys.

Soon it's reality,
for, during the scandal,
you could bet the big star coming out
of his head that Jerry Lee sees the song fighting back
for how he's been wronged,

as the uproar does some shaking on its own—
shaking his venues in each coliseum
into a cocktail lounge,
where he hunkers drunk
over a piano, tearing it
apart.

For years, he hits with
one-night
motel rooms
on the charts, finally
a longer stay
with "What Made Milwaukee Famous
Made a Loser out of Me."

On a turn-of-the-century tribute,
Mickey Gilley, his cousin, gushes
before Jerry Lee—that booted thistle—
trying on national TV
to flush out the rancor.

One moment they're together, the next
Mickey stands alone,
and you imagine
the legend at a stall
unzipping
just behind the rustling
curtain, then driving out
his spite
in the longest piss in Jerry Lee history.

Shelby Lynne, in Your Film Debut *Walk the Line,* You Seize the Blur of Johnny Cash's Mother

and walk a line all your own, give her flesh and bones,
make her a woman trying in silence
to keep every tree at its station
in the hours after losing her other son, Johnny's brother,
to the leaping blade of a table saw.
You show her colorless and composed, resolved
that nothing can be done. Though you are a firecracker,
we know the pain you borrow—a crack
in your family wedged in your driveway,
where there were cliffs for falling:
your father, the band man, without a glint
of music in his eyes, gnaws on a bullet,
tightens the old arguments,
kills your mother, then turns
the barrel's silver upon himself, you and your sister
watching. How, after that, you must
mother her, parent all pain, that poor child,
you keep skeletal in a closet,
so it does not grow into a monster,
while you prove there is yet silk
in the swish of a dress and look stunning,
adrift in rebel buoyancy apart from Nashville.
How strict your lunar glow,
as in *I am Shelby Lynne*, when you rasp
at the moon to reconcile you to a weepy gun
and to your pretty eyes that overdosed,
so that with you we find in your stir
of tones, asylum, a sway of grain
riding the gleam of night, and gain a foothold
on the dawn in that driveway where daily
you refuse to surrender to your own scream.

There Are Towns Where Streets
Have the Names of Songs?

New streets popped up like "I Want to Hold Your Hand,"
and there I was on the porch swing—
a shy boy clasping a girl's palm—
refusing to return it, despite hints in her cough
and, later, persistent but futile pulling;
neither of us uttered a sound.

For each street sweet-sounding as "Happy Together"
there were "Wedding Bell Blues"
and "The Worst That Could Happen."

And devious but alluring streets
like "Suspicious Minds," since Elvis had finally hopped
upon a tune worthy of his pipes,
a street weaving back and forth
where faces flattened against the windows
into shapeless forms.

When a girl from "It's My Party"
married a martyr from "Purple Haze,"
it was possible that the party could last
if the marriage didn't,
since opposites will collide in a kiss,
though their ears are always listening
across other streets.

Their parents agreed gladly,
when their kids moved out early to a street called "Beat It,"
taking with them that Michael machine,
beat street eater of the places
they had lived, chewing, since he owned it,
everything in the Beatles' catalogue.

I live safe on "Moondance" Lane,
where the moon serves my sentence of growing old.
I brush my mustache and beard with brown tone
and settle into the slow dance of my chair.

II

Kissing Was Everything

First, the dance, the mayhem of the catch
at 1 a.m., then to the car for carousels of kisses—
kisses whirling us over the top: the roller coaster, hair flying,
kisses heaving us from our seats, heads mixing it up
with the scuffed upholstery near the dome light,
our kisses making waves up the streetlights
on Marshall and out into the sky
toward WDGY in Bloomington, where
Boom, Boom Bailey, the deejay, was saying,
"I just got this vibe to play 'Palisades Park,'" later Boom Boom
spinning "Eli's Coming" by Three Dog Night,
then "Leaving on a Jet Plane" by Peter, Paul & Mary,
each hour's clinch pin in the spin rotation,
when "our bags are packed, ready to go,"
she kissing every boy in the whole wide world,
and I every girl. No braces,
though I sensed the jet plane in the slight metallic
aftertaste of gum, tongues diving, fluttering,
mine upon the lithe, succulent "l" sound in Valerie,
she a dorm-less girl kissing my lips somewhere
beyond me, her mouth a lighthouse warning to stay clear
of her heart. In "Leaving on a Jet Plane," dawn was breaking off
the night with a taxi's horn, giving each kiss an urgency
as an old man passed by walking his dog,
and the drugstore we parked by awakened light by light.

Hole in the Stocking

Oh, Joni Mitchell, from the start, I loved your phrasy glissades,
as in "You Turn Me On, I'm a Radio," the shimmering hang
of your heart—the impulsive poetry of "I'm a wildflower / waving for
you / a broadcasting tower / waving for you." And still,
when I was twenty-two, I winced at a line in a follow-up

hit that bit into the Top Ten—"Help Me," when you admitted
being wary of love in a tumble, when nationwide you sang
of a man who "danced with a lady with a hole in her stocking"—
that lady being you. Contrasted with me trying to hide craters,
what was a little hole in your panty hose?—though through my

own glossy heart, I wished not to see it. Then a boast undercut
your self-doubt with your taunting declaration: "Didn't it feel good"—
maybe more of a giddy bloom. Repeating it, you stretched
"goo-oo-ood" out for a clean six seconds, knowing what I'd
yet to learn—we love despite holes and because of them.

Already you'd sung of a child in "Little Green," your friends and fans
never guessing she was yours, a void left with no words to address it
when you gave her up for tugging, toothy tunes you nursed instead—
except holes in all that distance between high and low notes,
not only used to tote your tunes but fashion them. In light

of such canyons, producer Joe Boyd would say, "Most melodies now
are so constrained, so narrow. No one writes songs like that today."
No, you never avoided chasms, and maybe that is why
there are scintillating aural clouds in your voice, as if
sheer honesty had earned them, as in "Both Sides Now,"

the song's Ferris Wheel reeling a little, the song though, still composed—
you're not holding onto it by the knuckles—and that is why
when I think of you, I don't keep clouds in check, but let them fill
a hole in your stocking, while other clouds ease your high-pitched
cheekbones, fog in pale valleys and graze your neck.

.

As Space Junk Somewhere, the Old Songs are Floating

spinning slowly and looking like those discarded 45s
nobody rides in anymore, not the ones
that took young lovers to the stars,
some of them tunes that never
cut the Top 10, though they perfected
our hearts for maybe 3 minutes,
while they threaded through their grooves—
say "The River Is Wide," that overlooked gem
the Grass Roots played at The Roof Garden in Okoboji
in 1969. Dancing slow, my girl's cheek
against mine, the two of us inside the song,
as I played the sway of her lips for a kiss—
in my foray into paisley and the flow
of bell bottoms, she hiked up in her mini
just as the hook was climbing: "The river is wide,
the river gets long now" and for an instant
high in space, we're gazing down—
right through the roof at our weaving bodies
in a glow, to its left the midway
with its lowly Ferris Wheel and roller coaster
kidding the young they'll get where we are
in a few years—to its right, the cruise ship, *The Queen*,
where lovers touch off to Lulu's "Oh Me, Oh My,
I'm a Fool for You, Baby" or the Box Tops'
"Neon Rainbow," and for a second, I swear
we see that rainbow at our left, collecting itself in rows.
Soon we're looking to the west and down,
outside Estherville, a ballroom called the Skyline,
where my classmate Scotty's band is playing
"Your Love is Lifting Me Higher,"
and I'm up there with my baby
in a drifting whiz at 17,000 miles per hour,
like that space glove Edward White left up there
four years earlier, looking down
at those shiny ballrooms, the grinning horns
saluting us with a hand slide
that we have made it, her flowers all aflutter,

as we hold on tight and kiss
at the cloudy banister.

On a Road Some Saw as Washed Out

Into the bone of a microphone
Finn's voice scuffs it up like a Rhino's welcome.
No, a bull since it's Midwestern.
Piano-driven as Springsteen
and dressed in the dismay of Dylan, they play
like ghosts with calluses
about the boys and girls of America
having a sad time together.

Their songs swim the bass line;
the guitar's candor keeps them from coasting
as the Brooklyn band's pulsing waves
sweep through Kerouac into Finn's Minneapolis,
where they uncover desert. They witness fashion
chewed up by the calendar, emotion
beaten in the colanders,
druggies overdosing on drapes
and reaping ceilings, delirium unraveling
to homely laughter in the smoke of money,
where every child's an orphan.

The Twin Cities crashing against both coasts,
the band called Hold Steady gives witness
to those who live under the arching sensation of touch,
the kiss most empty of clothes.
Oh, the boys and girls
of America have such a sad time together.
And the band jumps the rain and rides it.

In the land of a thousand lakes
the boys want one to fish in.
The girls want to be lakes for them.
Everyone defines themselves by how little.
Wasn't it the new Gateway of America
the way the girls blindfold the mirror
or strike deep in it an image of themselves
for a place in the kingdom of the skin.

A little twist of lipstick and they're off again,
Finn sings now of Gideon, Holly,
and Charlemagne, all stricken stems.

His songs descend to the rising phoenix typewriter
of Berryman who jumped off the bridge
at Washington. In a nearby Deli
a young man feels the lunchmeat seep,
and knows he's not too cerebral for the full blowout bass
and meaty amplifiers of love.

His tires sing down Nicolette and Hennepin,
cruising after dark with his loose ends.
In one night, these girls are rubber bands
trying to hold a lifetime,
putting topspin on a kiss
that misses the boy for the mirror,
kissing an image of themselves in the mall,
for the mall is the new moon
shining down on them,
where everything slickens to their needs,
where death surely backs down.

They rise in dull escalator eyes
to the upper floor, looking for euphoria,
They giggle before the soft cudgels of clouds,
hip out braided walks in stiletto heels,
making their points about being cool
in the mall called America. And the band jumps
the rain and rides it.

Having Survived All the Open Mike Nights, Josh Ritter

both genial and small town, now opening act, tours alone
before releasing *The Golden Age of Radio.*
Far from Moscow, Ohio, his home,
after long hours on the road,
he motors his red Chevy Cavalier toward Manhattan.
Later, his car at a standstill, he looks for the justice
in a traffic jam, unfolds his bruised-up map, exits
the freeway, gets lost in the lean
of the New York streets. "Songs are engines
to solve problems," he believes,
and is fearful, has dream amalgams
of men who wait for him with tickets or tire irons,
and in the dark he can't tell who holds which.
He relies again on a dark, dark song to make
what he sees lighter through his side windows,
his ritual of singing Leonard Cohen's "The Future":
"Your private life will explode.
There'll be phantoms, there'll be fires on the road
and a white man dancing.
You'll see a woman hanging upside down.
Her features covered by her fallen gown,"
and as he steers into a turn, his car takes
a hard horn on the chin, and maybe after the concert
he's in his motel singing Cohen again,
but more softly now, as the thunder tunes up
and curtains swell with wind.

Yes, Laura Nyro, and at What River Did Her Piano Drink?

A dark river streaked with light, her voice a white cap
riding it for all it was worth after the debacle—
her shot at Monterey. A black journey of fabric flowing
to her ankles, she appeared as a bird gathering itself
into flight. "But I wasn't there," she would say,
at other times re-igniting rumor she'd been booed off stage,
until ten years after her death, when the Monterey film,
finally released, with its DNA, exonerates her.
But she who plunged into blooming
seclusion for two years as her lips would plunge
into the deepest red, let others have her hits, let the pop charts
go up the chimney, since she'd want chart purity
or nothing, unwilling to train her shrillness.
Instead in song she climbed the thinnest ragged slopes, digging in
gritty fingers of melody, barely clutching
love's unpardonable stone, or from a Mt. Everest
of love went falling, or her black gypsy hair jetting straight
back, her earrings still drinking from river glow,
she'd mount her rhythms, or they'd straddle her and together
they'd push one flesh note before the other—
in "Sweet Blindness," singing, "You're a good-lookin' riverboat,"
this song and others reaching the threshold,
to steam full breath or fall gloriously
apart, vocal chaos too unsettling for the sweetened
heartache of radio, as her voice dragged the sunset
for a gleaming spume of light.

Maris and Dylan Came Scowling Out of Hibbing, Minnesota

This town boasts the world's largest hole
and it bore through both of them.
Each had what the other did not,
traits stuffed, overgrown,
as if in the forty years that Hibbing moved south
and the Huff-Rust pit encroached,
things got mixed up: scent of dogs, mail routes;
gene pools split on couch, banister, and branch,
entering leaf buds
and x and y fell from the alphabet
or scored in throng.

Maris born for Pat Boone shoes
but no Pat smile, shoulders of the Mesabi range
while Dylan was born
in Hibbing at age six,
for leather jacket and boots,
and ducktails, no shoulders but a shrug.
And at Tiger Stadium,
before Maris hit his fifty-eighth home run,
he leaned against his bat
and watched Canada geese,
one large flock fly over;
it was the melting down of stone age man;
it was the sixties being born.
Dylan, born when his old self moved in from Duluth,
likely made concoctions in the pit
as boys are apt to do
whenever a fence's law breaks down.
When cells dislodged
as old Hibbing was overturned,
they came alive in contact with his skin
and each fish mouth nibbled a way in.

When Maris had looked up,
something deeper than home runs

held him like the white band does
across the goose's throat.
He squinted at the v-shape,
he who hated travel
from Kansas City to New York,
who made this leap because of Dylan
(Dylan's leaps were good for two)
who was nurtured in this soil
where houses, churches, saloons and stores
leaped each other for those forty years.

Maris stood outside the batter's box,
put off the cunning in this world,
put off the frowning Terry Fox, and Dylan wailed,
"I leap to Selma and Viet Nam,
I leap into the veins of leaves,
I leap into chlorophyll,
I leap into the mountain goat's horns
and turn them upside down."

Then Maris saw Hibbing as a shell-shocked town,
the courthouse crumbling, its windows blown.
And before he stepped in and hit the ball
into the upper deck in right,
just below where the geese had flown,
he glimpsed Dylan's myopic vision,
everything from Saigon to Hibbing
blurred into one,
and Maris leaped over gender
to a place where Dylan
raised ore dust in his throat and sang
and Maris tempered his distrust of the fans
in a place just the other side of music.

Elvis: The Great Comeback, 1968

With a slip of a shadow, he's on
the small, upraised stage,
out from under the strain of the Beatles,
a quiver he kills by making a fist.
The audience in a swim—mostly women—
as if thrilled that someone so pretty
can be a man. A toss
of his black leather hips
radiates light that Madison Avenue
turned into hula hoops
to teach white America to swing.

In a few years he'll need a girdle
to keep these hips garrulous,
but that's not tonight, as he leans in
to sing "That's All Right"—
with silky truculence
tongues his lips, giving topspin
to a kiss, while women drift through him,
leaving him unexpressed,
his hair twirled
around every woman's finger.

In Napoleonic collar, outside the halo
of his gospel roots, he feigns
being hunted: a pivot, percussive
bump, roll on the floor—
the women all the same to him,
so he flirts with his own pout and sneer,
as women pull him in with passion
unbeaten but made tender
in their loins, which travelling up, skips
the heart but boils down to stares
brought to a flame, as if stewing
flesh was a freer-wheeling gospel.

The "Get Back" Concert, Really

with Beatles holed up between chimney pots
and amps on the roof, Paul
a few growls into "Get Back,"
a barrage down the twist
of fire escape and over the London flats,
George and John, nearly Beatle dropouts, lean
toward the drop-offs. Ringo dreams
the cops will cuff this concert,
with the scraggly four
and carry it off, along with all that's fad
of being fab, as they skew the set list,
scurry through "Get Back"
three times, as even in the sky
they feel trapped: the roof, Apple studio,
the last public performance
if a mere coterie qualifies for public
and not just breezy
off the shingles, and if birds are public
curving in and out—
small airy things awaiting
the *White Album's* "Blackbirds," and if public
are the office girls in short skirts,
who just four years ago fainted
or gave chase, and they, too,
believe they hear a call
in the lift of an ear, and the piece of sky
they show above their knees
says they too are on the roof,
and the young clerks
now outside the haberdasheries
with windy triangulations of their ties,
look up as the chill
gives their eyes a glint of lust
and for the tune "Two of Us" Paul and John,
though they can't see
those long legs of girls
far below, feel their own faces swimming

among them in the silky nylons pulled
over the mikes
to keep the wind out.

After Your Tour with Dylan, You Finger the Strings, Lucinda Williams, and Sing "Lake Charles"

Up on the stage under a cowboy hat in a dance hall,
your pretty head is a sky
that carries its own clouds. Through your sleepy lips
I hear a voice so thin and frayed
it barely covers you. And even in a deadpan pose
you play it straight—singing about the man
who "had a reason to get back to Lake Charles,"
as if doing so could repair the sunrise:
no guitar fraught with fancy—as it quietly
smokes out a melody.

And though you make no mention of this,
I can almost see you and your friend
looking high into the sky over the courthouse
for your place in Lake Charles,
or coming in at the port of Calcasieu Parish—
the terminal with its flour and bagged rice
but not the two of you arriving on a hot blacktop
in that yellow El Camino that takes a road through your song.
And he turns to you with maybe his eyebrows ablaze
and says the line you sing,
as if going back could trim his shadow.

And, Lucinda, with wind in your heart as well,
maybe you, too, want to go back to Lake Charles,
you, this woman who looks like she doesn't have a home,
and older now, maybe like the man of whom you sing,
who comes off as at that age where
you fall out of the ranks of the handsome.
Then I think of you, Lucinda, while maybe
you hang up your nylons in an effigy,
and it's there you live, not the city of Lake Charles,
though you could coax it off like a blossom
any time in a song and hold it close
a moment before you let it go, as you tell me
in the grain of a whisper, you don't
write songs that nobody lives in.

A Year Before New Orleans
Is Immersed in Water

before city walls give way with a shrug,
Ray Davies, former front man of the Kinks,
walks with his woman
on the fringe of the French sector,
close to Bourbon Street, walks
from what some might call charming squalor,
flesh in leisure, maybe a little twist
of clouds in the sky. Surely, he looks older, surely
his hard edges now take soft journeys
down his jaw line, surely old songs
like "You Really Got Me" deaden his bloodstream.
But then it's that opening riff
all over again, when the power chords
nearly derail as a car stops in the middle
of the street, one thug at the wheel,
the other testing his mugger's luck,
creates haste with a shotgun
fresh in each face, snatches her purse
as if it's on clearance, the whole street sold
to darkness. And Ray, in his
prickly inequality from being at the top, explores
the bottom. Caution doesn't churn,
but instincts rush him, as he gives chase
to the mugger's small horizon,
before lead pummels him—
his right thigh leaping out behind,
leaving in one place his remainder.
Ray Davies, shaker of death,
at ease with being unsettled again,
down on the sidewalk, and not even sharing
the seed of a scream.

Leaning on His Gold Crutch

in rush-hour snow
of numb December
downtown
near the red light I'm stopped at,
a gray-haired man
in a smart gray overcoat
looking about as if
waiting for someone
and blowing on his fist
while snow whirls about his ankles,
who suddenly lifts the crutch
like a trombone
in his left hand,
and with his right as a slide,
thrusts it toward the overcast sky,
while his mouth
makes its mock trombone sound,
and he bends to each side,
sweetly gliding the slide
back and forth,
then seeing me unroll my window,
lowers his horn and sings
Chicago: "Does anybody really
know what time it is?
Does anybody really care?"—
then stopping cold,
replaces the horn, punches
it out five or six times,
before his lips pull back
from the make-believe
mouthpiece,
then grins wide and laughs
as if he'd knocked off a cloud.

Garage Sale

From a radio
across tables lazy with disarray,
on a day that may be realized in rain,
wafts "I Can't Stop Loving You."

The soothing strains have towed
the clouds away, affirming, too,
that love is in the aging. Browsing
the books and CDs, I am aware
of two women and a man,
each, like me, middle-aged, but unmindful
of the others, singing softly
with Ray Charles,
as if to vows sustained.

Honeyed by his song,
the sun finds what shines
in gloomy pans, sunken tins,
cupboards on the lawn.
And this fading man, balding
and wearing jeans, buoyed
by this song, by two women
and a man, the women
who've lost one beauty and gained
another, one holding
at arm length a skirt, lifting it,
like yesterday, into Ray's sweet song.

I see her now as younger,
one clothespin between her teeth,
another in her hand,
while her husband embraces her
from behind, just one sweet memory
she may have pinned to the line.

Before the song ends,
cryptic emblems on silverware handles

shall be understood;
days shall ripen on the vine.

At the Elvis Motel

you see him buckled into his pants
at the head of a longhorn,
billfold on a chain,
deep, pointed boots
as if to keep Elvis from falling out
as he keys the door.
You wonder what gradient of ghost he is.
His other hand has the motel by a doorknob.
Once it was the world.

He blows to you about recent hauls
to Montgomery and Memphis.
As if to beat you to the thought
he says that he
impersonates Elvis.
But noting all the bugs
about his head,
as if he is a streetlight
or the light of this world,
you dismiss it at once.

Later, in his room next to you
he is singing "Love Me Tender."
You imagine him flying
by his trucker-thick sideburns,
and wonder about pills
under his pillow
in this shabby motel
where TV is everything,
and carpet is mushed up
like milk toast.

You know you're just jealous
when you ponder
his wasted life
of poor songs and drugs,
so you kneel by the keyhole

to his door and inhale
snore after snore

until you hear a standing ovation
at Madison Square Garden
and he is saying you've
been a good audience
as if he's about
to slip back into his life.

The next day at check out,
the old clerk in a young ponytail
calls him Elvis, as if she doesn't know
who Elvis is.
But the trees outside fill
with birds as he walks to his rig
and wind feels gingerly
around his Styrofoam cup
of coffee
and blows him, holding it,
across the road
into dark plowed fields.

Back to the Bare Wire

Before overplay tempered it—
made it lie down forever as a song—
go back to "Fire and Rain,"
James Taylor's aching tenor
those first times to the end
when yearning stirs
to a Kitty Hawk—with "I always thought
I'd see you, Baby,
one more time again,"
the flying machine
reassembling. It's then Taylor sees her,
for you find yourself—
timepiece in hand—
running beside the plane
before the song ends,
where Suzanne's corpse willows,
her long hair flouncing a sparkle to her eye—
strange as the Wright's own
bicycle parts
learning the sky.

III.

When Van Morrison Scats

not the scatting when he runs
from an interview,
question one intrusive as
"How are you doing, Mr. Morrison?"
when wild-eyed as rain,
he feels the weight of the page
in the hand of a journalist
across from him,
stands up, pulling down
into his collar, and without a word
beats down a spiral of stairs,
his veins riled as he rattles the windows
all the way to the bottom door
of someone's opinion of him.

No, not *that* scatting, but the other
that reaches back to "Gloria,"
after the sweeping shout
of Gloria's name, the lines
"I'm gonna shout it to the night now"
and "I'm gonna shout it every day now"
come on with a lurch,
as if they were deadeye
improvised, and now we leap
a quarter century forward
to that Letterman show
when Van and Sinead O'Connor sing
"Have I Told You Lately" and Sinead,
with steady quiver, gives
his already sweet tune
an overly earnest reading, so Van,
understanding what's at hand,
punctuates with "Blah, blah, blah," extracting
all the unrelenting sap
and at the end, in his rooftop voice—
the opposite of fleeing—keeps
himself and us right there—his cheeks,

two depleting wind bags, as he
snarls, "You, you—
you, you, you, you, you!"

Dylan, the Low Years

At 49, in Tulsa, before the show, he leans back
against an amp, over his eyes tips
his hat to contemplation: knows that when he wants
he can fill a coliseum, that his concerts
won't be reduced out on the horizon
to the small shoebox tours
of Bobby Vee, who arrived with him on the scene,
and for whom he'd played piano
and longed to be like, ironically.

But something's wrong, and the critics
stick it to him: two- or three-star albums
when he used to have five.
Perhaps only the road and being 19 again—
his blood filled with blacktop—can give
back the old rush of faster stop signs,
and maybe the answer—oh hell, he'll have to
think it—is "blowing in the wind." Yes, feel
the wind in his sideburns again, steal
a petunia a few cellar doors from there,
find that Okie gal his heart says
isn't any older than she was thirty years ago,
and slip it behind her ear. Yes, this,
and not everybody's tired presence,
including his own, browsing the beat,
looking for the old Dylan.
Maybe start all over again in Minneapolis,
take the snow down University Avenue,
then later be the vender of dreams
in Greenwich Village, instead
of being marooned in the spotlight
or in the motel, that other spotlight,
the way he feels when he opens the drapes,
and still he overstays the key, so a clerk
has to tell him, "Tonight, Mr. Dylan,
your two suites are taken, reserved for someone else,"
while fame, that old woman, keeps dragging
a kiss across his face.

On the Usual Lark, Brian Jones, His Long Blond Hair in a Page-boy, Walks down Carnaby

the collar of his lace blouse splashing in his face.
He is weighted down by more than Berber jewelry,

this Rolling Stone, maybe drowning already—his head
aimed straight on this swimming street,

but his eyes swinging wildly, eager for a sign
that the girls emerging from boutiques like Lady Janes

and Take 6, or mincing toward him in minis
and leather boots, *know* who he is. To be this barmy,

as the other Stones say, this empty of the street:
the pubs, the eateries, the taxis, even a double-decker bus

screeching to a halt one inch from a tourist's face,
unmindful unless it impedes upon attention he receives,

oblivious, as he is to the quandary of the sky.
Yes, to walk out into the rough, a pied piper without

his clarinet, where the Carnaby shops are worked out,
of course, in doors, sensing that the Stones come down

to doors as well, and since Andrew Loog Oldham's
been on the scene, he feels pushed out of one:

he can smell the chlorine. His squat legs pumping slowly—
as if a howl is caught and he's swallowing it—

to walk out all flowery, where the wind fills in between
the buttons to tell him he can never be safe,

though he will always be free—this walking away
from the Stones and not knowing it, abandoning his guitar,

his sitar, his clarinet, his dulcimer, his many winged instruments,
for striding straight ahead, savoring the thought

of the first girl to jump him—her long legs angled
tartly below her skirt, each a clean whistle

of flesh and bone, then not look but keep walking.
The cry of another girl is culled to a whisper.

Now he's stepping faster, as fake black eyelashes
bat a pretty lass up and down. Another girl eddies

and taps her friend and—shoulder purses dangling—
they pursue him past Marlborough.

Glancing into his watery gait—as seen in a shop window—
he wallows in silhouettes of the girl train catching

up, imagines svelte mannequins in the window pining
to be picked up, or shaking themselves free

to "Have You Seen Your Mother, Baby,
Standing in the Shadows," imagines a big splash

of flying glass, then the buildup of one girl's shriek,
then another, and suddenly he's on the run—

followed by likely twenty girls (and the ghosts of three mothers
he left in his teens, each running with a baby

who owes, he figures a lot to him, babies, which,
in his mind, are still little pups). He never looks back

but darts ahead, then cuts over toward the Stone's office
on Regent, the young ladies plunging in a tidal burst

of brooding womanhood that has bone to aching bone—stewed,
waiting for a lone Rolling Stone to walk among them

in this Summer of Love, then to follow, chasing him up
and over the high cliffs and rocky path, struggling

with him in the steep descent, where immersed
in his celebrity, they try, like Brian Jones,

to catch their breath, then, like water, to keep running,
running to fill a pool, which in two years, will be ready.

Big Pink

Years with the Hawks, then behind Dylan's sneer,
with bellies full of hotels
they settle here in these Catskills
to compose and record. It's so private
one could shuck a curtain to its rod
so the house could go naked. In the basement
chairs are spaced out for playing room.
Of this split level the upper floor has what
is peaceful: the front door opens into the woods
where deer flare up in frolics and bear wear
a safe distance. Trees and leaves commit
themselves to touch, as does a pond
with its silk of fish. But downstairs
rush songs in deep breaths of country air,
or pleasant tickles in the arch
of the rib cage but also tough tunes
that release their interiors, like "Tears of Rage"
beaten into slow form by a faucet's drip
and "In the Station," where Richard sings,
"Out of all the idle scheming
can't we have something to feel?"—
but like their porous cinder block
letting weeds squeeze through the holes,
Robbie feels everything including
"the impossibility of sainthood—
that humans can never be good,"
though every oath shakes him
to his soul, and he carries Crazy Chester
and Fanny and the heaviness
of "The Weight" wherever they'll go,
even a few miles away to Yasgur's farm,
his eyes open to the notion that
even flowers can defile you.

At Madison Square Garden Springsteen's Voice Is Dressed in the Ghosts of Old Boxing Bouts

To a roadie in his corner he heaves his guitar.
Before it's grabbed, it hangs mid-air, a charge
in its shimmer. If not for the roof,
it would rise, as the Boss yells, "Move over,
Orion!" A ringing bell honors Chuck
Berry after intermission—the next round—
when the Boss, at 51, catapults
onto the piano, swaggers, then leaps
down into an intro,
its restless build up—fans waving forth
and back but never ducking
since they want to be pounded, numb
to everything from 9-11 to the 9 to 5.
But first the E Street Band with harmless punches
holds back. Nils Lofgren with guitar
and Clarence Clemons, carrying his sax,
with synchronized finger snaps
and a criss-cross of steps
in showy footwork.

Finally, the fans feel the Boss's undercut:
"Teardrops in the city,
Bad Scooter searching for his groove."
And no one thinks of the Bad Scooter
as Osama, though the Garden is in a flat-footed
dance as the fans yell "Tenth Avenue Freeze Out"
and weave in order to be hit
and flap at the elbows
in over-the-head clapping
or fist pumping flight toward the Boss,
who is all things, now a preacher
to their puffy hearts, as they rise
for the Boss's combination
in this interlude, a swing at the eternal,
which misses and clubs the fans instead,
a call for a rock'n roll baptism,

then in a nod to Marvin Gaye,
a plea for sexual healing,
the fans thinking, "Yes, hit me with that!"—
like Dylan fans, who never finding

what was blowing in the wind
also have a hungry heart.
But the Boss soon knocks
his fans gladly out—out of this world—
so that they're groggy like Patterson
KO'd by Liston in Chicago
decades before, in the seconds
afterward, when Patterson said, "It's a good
feeling actually, you're on a pleasant cloud,"
and feeling the crowd as family
circling, the Boss's fans, like Patterson,
right after the knockout, want to reach out
and kiss every woman and man.

Enough CDs for One Shelf

A CD or three a week—
easy to sneak into the house.
The first: Van the Man: *Astral Weeks,*
Moondance. A friend shakes his head,
says he's Vanned out,
while I soar for more
the stars have in store at Kaleidoscope Music.
Then it's *Meet the Beatles* all over again
thirty years later. Yeah, yeah, yeah!—
as I sneak home *Sgt. Pepper,*
Revolver, and *Rubber Soul.*
A second case in bloom,
I box up books to make room.
Soon the case surrenders,
and CDs establish posts
throughout the house: In the china closet,
Cat's *Catch Bull at 4*
on top. Nobody laughs;
the fake ice box where we keep cereal:
the snap-crackle pop of Bobby Darin
on the cover snappin' fingers
to "Mack the Knife."
Stacks leading up the stairs:
Pearls before Swine and the Velvet
Underground with Andy Warhol's banana
on the cover, still yellow,
but making it, along with the others,
up the stairs,

then into the bedroom,
where, between the bed and dresser,
in a pine case from a garage sale,
bootleg Dylans settle,
then landmark albums
I'd shunned, rare imports,
oddities, Pat Boone's
In a Metal Mood and the "Best of"

from artists I don't like
but think I should.

The case full, stacks rise
across its top, including soundtracks
like *Indecent Proposal*
and *Two if by Sea* picked up
for a quarter, until one day, I see,
to my horror, CDs cover the part of the wall
where my wife
in her wedding dress,
all hidden but her pretty head,
gazes up and away
as if even then
she saw this coming.

I Can't Get No

Mick Jagger pucker-mugs for the camera, agitating
Steve Allen, who'd tried to calm himself and the whirlwind

of history, so it would lie back down after he riled it
for his PBS show—*Meetings of the Mind*—

Allen, a charmed tunesmith, who'd write 4000 songs,
though as Jack Paar, who'd replaced him on *The Tonight Show,*

would say, "Name me *one!*" I'd have shot back,
"This Could Be the Start of Something Big." Steve Allen,

knowing his worst song was better than "Satisfaction,"
for four decades had railed against the Stone's song,

with a sneer that matched Jagger's, as he pondered the
frontman's own response to the tube: "When I'm watching

my TV / and a man comes on and tells me,
how white my shirts can be / well he can't be a man

'cuzz he doesn't smoke / the same cigarettes as me,"
and Jagger knows, of course, that it's folks like Steve Allen

whose white, white shirt is always judged perfect by a black bow tie.
Something *is* funny when the comedian in Allen smirks at

"Satisfaction"—that song he knows is rubbish, then recites
Keith Richard's lyrics, as if they were Shakespeare's,

but with mock passion: "I can't get no satisfaction, /
'cuzz I try and I try and I try and I try / I can't get no…"

and thinks of Jagger's big lips and androgynous fuss
of facial contortions and tells the Stones how white

their songs should be, Mick with lipstick flicked on, mirror-
ing the girl he wants to hunt down, and Steve Allen,

actor and writer, with one Emmy and a Peabody and TV
Critics Award and a film Advisory Board Award, is *not*

acting when he dies the next day after publishing
a full-page diatribe in newspapers throughout America

concerning the changing culture, which, of course,
Jagger and the Stones, in England, do not read.

Okoboji—the Back Lobby of the Holiday Inn

the ache of late afternoon, before the band
played the Roof Garden, I spied
the lead guitarist. He'd just reached
into the pop machine for a can that clunked down,
and I had that instant finished mopping.
Smiling about something, his grin traced
the mop handle up to my face as he turned
around. I told him how good his band jammed
the night before, this rock group that ranked
with the Fabulous Flippers, Mad Dogs,
and Quarrymen, other bands with a big
Midwest following but without any hit.
He wore jeans and a Nehru shirt.
In hours he'd be afflicted with flamboyance—
a blouse, buffed up, all ruffles
and glitter—maybe twenty buttons
running down, shoulder pads,
sequined slacks and red sports jacket.
He smiled again, and then asked about me.
When I shared my plans for attending
the seminary, his eyes glowed a moment,
and then looked down, said he'd love
to trade places but wouldn't wish his life
on anyone, offered that he'd abandoned
his values for drugs and a broader squalor;
there was no pulling back from girls
who'd do anything they'd do
for the Rolling Stones but faint for him.
He was matter of fact. Bit by envy,
I didn't try to save him but watched him
leave, then took a swipe with my mop
at something that looked
a lot like hope, then thought
that even if my heart were right,
what to do with a shrewd eye
that saw what he had and wanted it.

On My Knees, Poking a Paintbrush
Where the Ground Meets the Base of the House

thinking while blaring
Van Morrison's "Wavelength"
how bearable
Father's final breath was,
compared to last year when
his labored inhalations shook
his hall,
and exhalations
the hospital's 3rd floor. Suddenly
a thin, precise
shrillness
screams up from
beneath the bristles,
louder than Van from an insect
I can't see, what should have died
quietly—if the history of swatting
and brushing away tells me
anything, the wave of all hurt
evening things out,
the symmetry of the scream
widening for seconds,
then tapering
to a beam. I bear down
on the bristles,
snuff it out, shudder and paint on,
not thumbing through
the fur of dirt.

Jeff Buckley Sews His Voice to the Seamless River

Maybe a splash of melody
and into the Mississippi
he walks, fully clothed,
near Mud Island Harbor at sunset.

Just outside of Memphis,
where he laid down tracks in the studio,
he sets down his final ones with his boots,
in his Altamont t-shirt, wading deep
into "Whole Lotta Love,"
singing it high and surely wide.

His high, wavering lungs match
the ghostly operatic voice
of Tim Buckley, his father.
A passing river boat crests waves
upon his cheeks;
his friend on the shore
who'd turned back, spins around
and Jeff Buckley's gone—
the current's breach already healed,
no call for help—an immaculate departure—

as if his voice, that lonely mansion,
found itself on another shore,
as if he'd carried in him a secret
known only to the bearded trees
and silken moon, his death sweet
as the lilac wine beneath the linden trees
in one of his songs, and then to keep
his death pure and not a drag
upon the river, a dense and lengthy showcase
of rain appears before his body is found
as a floating neglect of his spirit
out in the reaches, where we teeter.

Before Maybe an Apocalypse, a Singer Lives in a Huge Rented House, Not Minding Trips to the Laundromat

where he savors coffee, extracts from shadows
of conversation he listens in on, ideas for a song.
Ron Sexsmith, who under a big bush of brown hair,
at 47, an age that mirrors late autumn's sudden dusk,
rides the bus of his yet boyish face.

Recently he answered an apologetic post on craigslist,
by saying, "It really wasn't a big deal. All is forgiven."
His songs lauded by McCartney, Elton John, and Elvis Costello,
he's resigned to probably being born too late to have
a hit song, yet ten albums onto his dry dirt path, on gales
of delicate melodies, he strives for one.

The night before his own post, this rarity: ridicule
from a drunk fan who'd called him asshole
and more for wearing an echo shirt:
"Mr. ron sexsmith," her post began, "im so sincerely
sorry for quite possibly ruining your evening.
im on this medication, I shouldn't drink. i did."

Ron Sexsmith, watching the whirl through the window
of a dryer, this shy, self-effacing man whose eye catches
on a shirt, the small wings of a collar,
on which a song may become airborne,
who comes alive on stage, a crooner absorbed in
the smaller things, maybe one of these days
the street life of a leaf or a raindrop twitching down
a woman's face, as the dry, dry lint in a laundromat
becomes fodder for some lyrical spark.

I first came upon him in a Youtube video: Bay Street in Toronto,
where along with the lead singer of the Barenaked Ladies,
he backed up and prompted Leonard Cohen
in a rousing version of Cohen's "So Long, Marianne,"
applause gusting in the wind of each refrain
on a day that struck a cloud opening for everyone,

but now five years later, the world about to be pushed
over the edge, the washers and dryers rocked too hard
or on their sides for an earth that's maybe nailed down
its last dawn, Ron Sexsmith refuses to give in
to the syndrome of dull laundromat eyes,
but in a painterly haze is holding on.

Over the Clatter of Plates, The Four Seasons Sing "Oh What a Night"

and I'm looking under tables in morning light
or booths shunned to shadow.
In the same strangeness as twice last week,
I'm peeking at an old codger's feet
while maybe Felix Cavaliere of the Rascals has me
swooning to "Groovin' on a Sunday Afternoon."
Maybe the old man's wife drums up music
of things to do at home, and he's at the café
showing a shock of bare leg between jeans landing
way too high and white socks that barely climb
the ankle's hobble—that very public skin
that matches his vacant eyes, as if both
shades are drawn. Yes, I watch
below that unsavory terrain for toe-tapping
to a tune from the speakers—
another early morning loner who I hope, like me,
still has something to feel.

Sometimes I'm desperate even
to find below that span of pale skin
any foot—shoed and not so far gone—
still some faithfulness in that
old floor tapper. I'm not fussy
about rhythm either, for there's homely charm
in a foot lagging a beat behind
in that sweet fumbling with no follow through.
And sometimes, when the foot fails, a fist
will knuckle down for maybe Dion's "Runaround Sue,"
beat out an old forgotten flame on a tabletop—
dancing a phrase tarnished and worn, without
the gleam of silverware
slid to the side to find room.

No Organ Player, Al Kooper Storms the Empty Hammond to Give a Song Its Signature Sound

But first, from urban scurry he slips
into the studio as winds wail, filling his white shirt,
flapping his tie; he unsheathes his guitar like he
belongs. When the organist shifts to piano,
his bench becomes the new benchmark for empty,
Kooper, careless as always with uncertainty,
cons the moon and stars,
eases into that seat as naturally as a yawn,
to show that he belongs.
It is rearranging tusks on an elephant
to feel he can own these ivories,
but that primal gnawing unearths the organ's sound
as Dylan behind sunglasses,
with truculence groans the wild brush:
"Once upon a time you dressed so fine,
threw the bums a dime, in your prime,"
the song dented up by drums,
then mixing it up just short of dust,
and Kooper, with fingers left over from the cave,
with the Hammond bone clubs the next meal,
the girl Dylan sings about with a hunger
that can't be shaken out in some discotheque,
stands in wilted shoes
as Dylan snarls and his voice writes lessons
in the dust, and Al Kooper feels
the pull of the earth, that eternal repertoire,
on keyboards writes the new hieroglyphics.

It's Not That Your Clock Got Lost, Neil Young, and Took You Back Thirty Years

You've never stopped rocking the outer reaches,
your guitar never a moment on safety.
At the Van Andel in Grand Rapids
for a reunion tour with CSN&Y in 2002,
roadies, a step ahead of me in the wide corridor,
told fans at their elbows they'd chalk a circle
on stage to keep you in place, Neil,
so you wouldn't butt up against
the other band members when your body wielded
in a ragged pivot of your boot heel
while rocking through everything from "Let's Roll"
to "Rockin' in the Free World," your stringy shoulders
trying to turn your back on everyone at once.
Smoke doesn't take well to being fastened,
you learned long ago, growing up in Toronto,
your greasy hair, smoky and long at the sides
with a crewcut on top, your heart
in whatever shape haste will make it through scruffy,
impassioned play and rash exits, as in '67,
when Stills was with you in Buffalo Springfield.
Right before you were to glaze the night on Carson,
you quit the group, denying that big flash
of coruscating light. The current group knows
everything must be built around *you*, the only one
still with star enough to make big bucks surrender—
the group never to tour with just your shiny absence.
So, there you stand, looking out from the inside
of *Mojo* magazine and wearing the horizon
in your funny hat, with no wind to snatch it
because it's all in your heart.

"Walk Away Renee" Writer Worn Down
by His Overworked heart, a Pumping Wonder

i.

thumped through unrequited. My hunch, Renee, is that in your elusive
west coast whereabouts, you hear the news but only look on,

as you did from the control room in the New York
recording studio in '66, where, his nervous author hands

fumble the harpsichord part—easy to understand with you
looking on, when lyrics stick to a relationship with you that—

to his embarrassment—did not exist. "Just walk away, Renee,"
declares Michael Brown. "You won't see me follow you back home."

My brother and I and friends in Iowa long ago, Renee,
stirred crazy about a girl like you—so it's easy to see how

every member of the Left Banke loved you:
Michael, 17, writing you into songs feathered out

in three-part harmonies by others in the band;
Steve Martin with the sad wings of singing lead;

George Cameron, tumbling in his drums for you
down a flight of stairs, a descending chromatic bass melody

played by Tom Finn, your boyfriend, who must have sensed
he'd last no longer than a hair rinse;

Rick Brand, guitarist, who joined the band just in time
for P.R. photos, just in time for you, Renee.

ii.

Through the lit skull of imagination stars fall and rise again:
Michael Brown must have imagined

that when you stood by the "sign that points one way,"
your blond ponytail, rising through your hair band,

was a fountain springing forth in the wilds.
Even amidst the band's in-fighting, with Michael hardly

knowing you but as he put it, "mythologically in love,"
his pain purer, fonder since your lips, Renee, never

grazed his own, unlike the lips of Finn, the bassist,
who, in 2011, tried to revive the group around your hymn.

iii.

In 2015, Michael dies one day after he finally inks
a contract to mingle again with the moon,

though "Walk Away, Renee" won't again be in rotation
with the planets. Oh Renee, even if you're no longer

the "Pretty Ballerina" of your leggy form, summon
your inner grace to graze over the truth, bringing Michael

and his harpsichord heart back to us, while I raise a candle
to the Iowa girl spirited off not long after she gave

our lives a whirl. And, light your own for the shy, sensitive boy
resigned to stand back and not call you out as others might

in this vulgar age, but politely watch you walk away.

Driving the Queen through the Homecoming Parade in Terril, Iowa

Basically, Barb, it was you and the convertible;
I was alone, though you'd chosen me as your attendant,
I sometimes looking down at my tie
and thinking about how in a blind act you missed
in pinning a tail on a donkey, as I skirted
the potholes and aimed for once
for the middle of the road, you smiling broadly, waving
at everyone and no one as queens are apt to do,
having forsaken the usual small-town tears,
unlike other such girls who break down, believing
their beauty suffered so much to get there,
you no longer mine after school at the cafe,
where we'd meet and you'd slip in a dime
and play "Green Grass on My Window."
Our days were history, though how resplendent
you were to retrieve me from nothingness,
so I could drive you beneath the maples
with all their arboreal charm, your old boyfriend
your new one again and that afternoon driving
home from the university for the dance,
while here at the parade, you were seated,
where on cue the roof had pulled
back to give you room, trying to puff you up
beyond your bouffant. You didn't budge
from who you were, though the backseat
was your foot well, the slit of your dress
a flash of thigh that said all was right in heaven,
and I driving you beneath the music
of the trees, lost in my gathering neglect—
all the times I never fought once to keep you—
and remembering when I, too, tasted royalty,
above our long straws over the Cokes
that we shared, straws that lifted us up,
even if not in the way of those wooden poles
that carried a king and queen through ancient streets.

Leonard Cohen Knew That, at the End, We're All Astronauts

Even at 78, as *Old Ideas* reached #1
in ten countries, his stage life still streamlined
right down to his trim suit and tie flashing
the old aerodynamics,
his fedora's brim, on his 2012 world tour,
like those tailfins on '62 Fairlanes, or spaceships
rocketing in the decade awaiting the first lunar prance.
Four years later, at 82, with his final album release,
he smiled that he was ready to go.

He'd already strapped on the large, floating helmet
of the universe. Had his humor flowed
into air tubes to the future,
it might have noted he'd beat John Glenn,
who'd die in December, off the launch pad by a month,
his glint of eye reminiscent
of two decades before when he joined Tibetan monks
on Mt. Baldy, and if the monks attained
a spiritual peak, they still cast themselves
as a net beneath Leonard.

On Baldy, he'd found sanctity in even his small kitchen pans,
cooking for one, then again in the washing,
maybe scrubbing away, too, at "his celebrity, his success,"
things, he said, that "he could never locate."

Leonard lived as though he could not forget
that raindrops fall back upon their dust.
But as he aged, he grew unhindered by
the gravity of doom
as he'd head into the unknown.

Once seeing a raving beauty seated with her party
at a restaurant, he walked up and requested a clip of her hair.
Embarrassed as she was, she assented,
and he scissored it, and right there dunked the strands

85

into his crystal glass of wine, maybe a rich,
red Mediterranean, which he then expressed
upon his tongue in an early lift-off,
another kind of singing.

How to Take That Smoke Ring Back

that poised spiral with a bluish-gray hue
that skirted the high freight of your cheekbones,
then lassoed your pretty nose
after you showed me up, and I drove
to the Roof Garden alone, only
to spot you that night in animal hours
that the two sexes brushed by each other—
you in the throng that circled
clockwise, me in the one walking counter—
Pat Upton and his Spiral Starecase performing
"More Today Than Yesterday" and me
with no *today*, young people primitive
in their flipping through of each other,
as with clothes racks on sidewalk sales.

Inside the perimeter lovers dancing,
and I envious of that wonder,
found you suddenly in the throng, caught
your eye, then stepped in close—
your lashes flashing, eyes widening, watching
the vulnerable wobble I blew come for you.
Not one of your hands raised to ward off that ring,
with you maybe afraid it would slip onto
your finger—this just a week after I met you,
my hometown, Terril, about ten miles
from your Milford. Remember? We'd shared
the last two dances—one fast, one slow.
I am sorry. I should have known
the boys with brooms were already out.
I'd invoke that heavenly body
for the ruins there, relieved for any blur
you could bring, for sometimes my mind
with aplomb still puffs that floating ring.

But I want to turn it around, choke
on that Platters' song that was before our time,
"Smoke Gets in My Eyes," not ever wanting

that ring of smoke to slip—kiss-precious—
from my lips. For five decades, I've zeroed in
on your quiver, in cacophonous dust
your eyeshade darkening in some desire.

The Clay County Fair is Calling Me Home

for Johnny Rivers, near 70, to take a ride on the rockabilly
decades after his heyday, still holding his own
in the uplifted eye of the town of Spencer,
where a Ferris Wheel prevails for a week each September.
Let the grandstand slow his blue-eyed soul
born of a sky hanging blue among the trees
in sunny Iowa, where folks will toss up an idea,
then feel the wind warmly wheeling it about.

Forty-four years ago, my steps wove through Midway,
music everywhere, not only in the grandstand
but the screened-in pie stand, where sweet meringue swirled up
and sang, the cream pie I'd eat always rising to #1,
like "Poor Side of Town," all over that autumn with Johnny pining,
"To him you were nothing but a little plaything,
not much more than an overnight fling,"
which I misheard as "overnight flame," light left untamed,

with Midway's many lights melting into midnight—
no matter the hour, and me in the shadows
of his *Changes* LP, imagining I'm handsome like Johnny
on the cover, winning back my girl in the dark
in a year the fair could have never lured Johnny
out riding moonbeams after a run on the Sunset Strip,
lighting up the Whiskey A Go Go with "Maybelline"
and "A Mountain of Love," which I learned

this spring before they lay Harmon Killebrew,
Twins' slugger, in the ground, was the Killer's favorite song,
leaving me to long even more for the calm waters of Johnny's tenor
soothing ears recoiling from the tune of the tractor pull,
the rising octaves of the raceway screaming I haven't been
to the fair since I was lifted up that final year,
when a waitress with a broom asked me to raise my legs
so that she could sweep, and being too slow I was swept up, up,
and out of there, over the Spook House and Ferris Wheel.

Acknowledgments:

I am grateful to the editors of the following publications in whose pages the poems in this book first appeared:

Asheville Poetry Review, Common Ground Review, Concho River Review, The Courtship of Winds, Driftwood, Entropy, Gravel, Great Lakes Review, Iodine Poetry Journal, Passages North, Poet Lore, Spillway, and *Twyckenham Notes.*

"Maris and Dylan Came Scowling Out of Hibbing, Minnesota" first appeared in *New Poems from the Third Coast,* published by Wayne State University Press and edited by Michael Delp, Conrad Hilberry, and Josie Kearns.

"Driving the Queen through the Homecoming Parade in Terril, Iowa" first appeared in *Song of the Owashtanong: Grand Rapids Poetry in the 21st Century,* published by Ridgeway Press and edited by David Cope.

"Since You Always Threw Yourself Out There, David Ruffin" first appeared in *Poetry in Michigan / Michigan in Poetry,* published by New Issues Poetry & Prose and edited by William Olsen and Jack Ridl. The poem also appeared in *Respect: An Anthology of Poems on Detroit Music,* published by Michigan State University Press and edited by Jim Daniels and M.L. Liebler.

"No Organ Player, Al Kooper Storms the Empty Hammond to Give a Song Its Signature Sound" first appeared in *Visiting Bob: Poems Inspired by the Life and Work of Bob Dylan,* published by New Rivers Press and edited by Thom Tammaro and Alan Davis.

"Catching What's Cool: Holiday Inn in Okoboji, Iowa" first appeared in *Local News: Poetry about Small Towns* edited by Tom Montag and David Graham.

"With the Hard Band Rocking off for the Weekend" was first printed in *Home: An Anthology of Minnesota Fiction, Essays, and Poetry,* published by Flexible Press and edited by William Burleson.

Hearty thanks are given to Russell Thorburn for inspiration, feedback on individual poems and assisting with their ordering in the manuscript. Thanks, also, to David Allan Evans, Barb Saunier, and Robert Haight for many years of helpful critiques, also to Miriam Pederson and Alyssa Jewel for input on several of the later poems.

Grateful tribute is extended to Johan Vandertol for the book's cover design.

Poet **Rodney Torreson** grew up on an Iowa farm. According to the Poetry Foundation, "His plainspoken yet mystical poems draw on the landscapes and traditions of the Midwest." In 1986, he earned an MFA from Western Michigan University. *The Jukebox Was the Jury of Their Love* is his fifth book. In addition to two other full-length collections, *A Breathable Light* (New Issues Press, 2002) and *The Ripening of Pinstripes: Called Shots on the New York Yankees* (Story Line Press, 1998), he has published two chapbooks, *The Secrets of Fieldwork* (Finishing Line Press, 2010) and *On a Moonstruck Gravel Road* (Juniper Press, 1994).

The former poet laureate of Grand Rapids, Michigan, Torreson won the *Seattle Review*'s Bentley Prize, and Storyline Press named him runner-up for the national Nicholas Roerich Prize for first books. He was also a finalist for *Spitball Magazine*'s Casey Award given for the best baseball book of the year.

Torreson lives in Grand Rapids with his wife Paulette, where he taught at Immanuel-St. James Lutheran School for thirty-six years. In 2007, he created the online youth poetry journal *Through the Third Eye*.